Introduction

This book is designed to help you direct your own recovery plan.
to get to know you better, and help them and other people involved in your recovery to ~~g~~
to see how you want your life to be and understand how best to support that.

The key person is you, which means you are the most important person in this process – your needs, wishes and hopes are vital to the process.

It is important that you are the person responsible for deciding the information recorded as it is the starting point for making decisions about your future, and helping us to provide the services you want and need to support you in your recovery.

Wherever possible, the form should be filled in by you in the language which you feel comfortable with. Take your time to think carefully and record everything you think is important. This form should be filled in over a period of weeks after you and your assessment worker have begun the Individual Planning process.

The assessment worker will discuss each category with you in depth and then write a summary at the end of this form which together you should agree upon. The two parts form your Recovery Plan.

If at any stage you feel uncomfortable with what has been previously recorded about you, it is your responsibility to discuss this and any required changes to the form with your assessment worker.

Remember the more information you give, the better it enables people to support your recovery in the way you determine.

Recovery following distressing experiences can be a seemingly complicated phenomenon that is described in complex language by many people. In reality however there are a number of underpinning focal elements that are the foundations for personal recovery and moving on to find a future and build your resilience.

For comfort and ease of navigation we refer to these underpinning elements collectively as THRIVE©. They come in no particular order, have no greater merits than as a descriptor and are no more or less important than each other.

Throughout the Recovery plan, as you fill in the different sections. it may be useful to reflect on each of these themes and consider them in relation to your journey of recovery.

The THRIVE Approach - The 6 underpinning factors

TIME is a natural healer as long as we don't resist the process and become stuck. Think of someone you have loved who has died. The pain of grief becomes less raw over time – you don't forget or stop missing the person, but over time you focus on the joy of knowing them rather than the pain of losing them. So it can be with emotional problems.

With time, you will feel differently, gain a different perspective and move away from the distress you feel right now. In depression it is important to remember this, to have hope and belief that things will get better. Obviously hopeful attitudes are difficult to maintain in the depths of depression but we will explore ways of reclaiming hope, explore how to "reframe a situation" and how others can be our "holders of hope"

Time limits are not helpful to you. Don't feel pressurised by others into making progress in a definitive way, i.e. achieving certain things within a certain time frame. This will only increase your depression. It is more important to work at your own pace and in your own way, building things up slowly and surely. This will sustain you in the future, particularly in the face of future difficulties.

HEALING is integral to recovery and essential to everyone's wellbeing, sometimes easier to impart to others than to give to ourselves. There may be reasons why we block our own healing – guilt, worthlessness, shame, lack of belief in our own worth. Part of the healing process is to acknowledge these emotions, and allow healing elements into our consciousness. Learning to know and accept ourselves for who we are is crucial to the healing process and the book explores ways in which this self knowledge can be accrued.

Often the reasons for distress have built up over a long period of time; therefore the healing process equally may take a long time. Different ways of helping the healing process along are considered in the workbook – some will work for you better than others. It may be worth trying all of them, even if you are sceptical that they will work for you – you may get a surprise!

Showing **RESILIENCE** is a common factor in those who have survived and rebuilt their lives. Indeed we all have a degree of resilience, and some people are able to draw on their inner reserves and show resilience even where the system attempts to squash it. It is also possible to build up our own resilience and to help support the process in others.

Building resilience and learning a range of effective coping strategies is a vital element of recovery, helps to maintain wellness and may be important in preventing future setbacks.

By learning how to overcome negative emotions it is often possible to predict and avoid subsequent bouts of depression.

Often people make the mistake of striving for total independence. This is not realistic – we all rely on other people for some things some of the time, and other people may rely on us.

A healthier attitude is to look at ways of increasing our personal connections and relationships, building circles of **INTERDEPENDENCE**.

Many people are great at helping others and being strong allies and supporters for others, not as good when it comes to themselves. It may be that your depression has driven people away or you have tended to shut yourself away from others because you are depressed.

In the long run this will increase and worsen any negative feelings, therefore it is important to acknowledge your needs for support, companionship and activity and take responsibility to build these into your recovery.

VIVACITY is not a term we hear very often in mental health spheres, (ironically if you show aspects of vivaciousness or signs of enjoying life in-between periods of psychic distress you might be mistaken for being manic and acquire a label of Bi-polar Disorder!) Our conviction is that we should be thinking about exuberance for life as a vital part of recovery.

Although psychic distress can be disabling and energy draining and it feels as though you never can be interested in anything ever again, it is possible to resurrect feelings of pleasure. Having a lust for life, being animated, full of the joys of living is possible for all.

Many people who have experienced severe lows in their lives talk about enjoying life even more after coming through their distress. The friendships you forge in adversity tend to be based on mutual respect, affection and consideration, and as the saying goes, "All that doesn't kill us makes us grow".

Many people who recover talk about feeling "Weller than well", that is, they appreciate their lives even more because of previous adversity.

EMANCIPATION or liberation comes with taking control of one's own life and celebrating your own individuality and uniqueness.

Playing a vital role in society and being valued can enhance our sense of freedom and remove us from the constraints of being regarded as mentally unwell, maintained in the system and feeling life happens to other people.

Being in the mental health system, for some people can be very addictive and there may be rewards to remaining unwell. It can be a source of comfort to have others to rely on, to look after our needs and it can also be an excuse to stop us doing things which we secretly fear.

However, it is only by moving out of the comfort zone, the "self-imposed prison" that we truly free ourselves and take control of our lives. This involves hard work but the benefits are well worth it.

There is a famous saying, "The journey of a thousand miles starts with a single step"
Our take on that is if you're still standing, you're already on the journey!

General information about me

My name is:

I like to be called:

My date of birth is :

My address is:

I have lived here for (years):

My key worker is called:.

My care co-ordinator (if different)is called:

My last care plan meeting was held on:

These forms were completed by myself and:

They were completed on; (date)

My next care plan meeting is to be held on:

**The people I would like to invite to my next care plan meeting are:
(a tick indicates they have been invited)**

**Myself
Assessment Worker
Advocate
Family Members
Others (list names)**

I would like the meeting to be held at:

I would expect the meeting to last approx:

Part One – Me as an individual
The information given here will help your worker to build up a picture of who you are as an individual - your personality and your preferences, but most importantly your skills and strengths.

How I feel generally at the moment:

Things I like (doing) at the moment are:

Things I used to enjoy but don't currently enjoy:

Things I dislike (doing) or have fear of (doing) at the moment are:

Things I am good at are:

Things that I feel proud of include:

What I like about myself:

Things others like about me:

Part Two – My Interdependence / Connectedness to others

One of the prerequisites to good health is the ability to feel connected with others. This extends beyond our inner, intimate circle of people who we love and who love us, but embraces a wider group of people who we feel connected to in some way. This could be through a shared passion, e.g. a sport, music, cinema, theatre, educational courses or through a shared bond or experience.

My regular routines at the moment consist of:

In a typical week I do the following things:

	Morning	Afternoon	Evening/Night
Monday			
Tuesday			
Wednesday			
Thursday			
Friday			
Saturday			
Sunday			

During a typical week day I do the following things:

When I get up I:

At breakfast I:

During the mornings I:

At lunchtime I:

During afternoons I:

At tea time I:

During evenings I:

At the end of the evening I:

I usually go to sleep at:

I would describe my days as:

I would describe my sleeping patterns as:

The local places that I use are listed below.
I have also ticked the ones I would like to use more

Place	Use Once a week	Use Once a month	Use less often	Like to use more often
Shopping centre				
Local shop				
Evening class or college				
Cinema or Theatre				
Clubs				
Pubs				
GP				
Place of worship				
Restaurant				
Work				
Sports centre				
Park				
Library				
Leisure centre				
Clinic				
Others - list				

What prevents you accessing the above more?

How could you be supported initially to access more of the above?

Part Four - My Relationships

People (or animals) who rely on me

I have good relationships with:

I don't have very good relationships with:

Others describe me as:

Sometimes I do think or say things which can cause other people problems including:

I get my feelings across by:

The problems I have in letting other people know my feelings are:

I am trying to improve the way I get my feelings across by:

Part Four - Recreation, Leisure

I like to relax by:

In my spare time I:

List the things that you are passionate about in your life:

Are you able to enjoy these things as frequently as you would wish? If not, why not?

The things I have never done but would love to try include:

I would be interested in taking part in; (tick as many as you like)

Football	Badminton
Singing	Table Tennis
Keep fit	Climbing
Theatre	Dominoes
Cinema	Climbing
Dancing	Yoga
Rambling	Orienteering
Archery	Hockey
D.I.Y.	Martial Arts
Fishing	Sailing
Music	Bowling
Golf	Cricket
Tennis	Pool
Cycling	Squash
Abseiling	Darts
Snooker	Drama
Bingo	Sports
Acting	Swimming
Horse Riding	Rugby
Model making	Aromatherapy
Weight training	Athletics

Part Five - Meaningful Occupation / Work

My thoughts about work:

The support I would need to work includes:

If I felt I could be supported in work, I would like work which involves:

The benefits/allowances I receive include:

Work I have done in the past (including voluntary work) includes:

Skills / abilities which would be useful (e.g. caring, budgeting, computer skills, people skills) include:

Part Six - Education

If you had the opportunity to learn something new, without it affecting your benefits, what might you be interested in? For example - something creative, a skill, something academic, music, painting.

I would like to further my education and learn more about:

The type / level of course which would suit me is:

The difficulties I might face include:

The support I would need includes:

The length of course I think I could cope with:

Qualifications I already have, exams passed etc.

Part Seven - Physical Health &Wellbeing
In terms of my general health I have had/need regular checks on: Please record dates.

Chest x-ray
Bloods
Physical Examination/BP
Dietary Advice
Eyes
Ears
Breast Cancer Screening
Others...........................

The health problems that I have are:

I get the following treatments:

In the past, I had the following health problems:

In the past, I had the following treatments:

I am trying to keep /improve my physical health by:

I take medication/tablets for:

I have taken this for:

The effects are:

My views on the medication are:

What I would like to happen regarding medication:

Part Eight - Spiritual / Cultural Needs

Many people find that development of their own spiritual beliefs about life can prove helpful to their recovery. Questions such as "Who am I? What am I doing here? Where am I going? What does it all mean?" may be more meaningful when placed within a spiritual or a religious context.

People need to remember special things about my culture/religion including:

My beliefs include:

Things of special significance to me include:

Things I do to express my beliefs / culture:

Things I do not wish to do (or wish others to do) because of my cultural or spiritual beliefs include:

Things that would be offensive to me include:

Things that would upset me include;

Things me people could misinterpret as illness include:

Part Nine - Family and Friends

My close friends and family members are:

I see them:

List each persons name below	Every Day	Once a week	Once a month	Less often

My circles of Support

Use the large circle on the next page, spiraling out from the centre with 5 areas. Number them from 1-5 with 1 in the middle, then, following the instructions write the names of people you know in the appropriate areas 2-5. You are number one!!

Filling in the Circle of Support

1. The focus person – you
2. The circle of intimacy for loved ones and those especially close to you, for example best friend, family members
3. The circle of friendship for good friends, pals, and mates you can count on
4. The circle of participation or association , those with whom you share an interest or whom you meet for an activity, for example a club or church you attend
5. The circle of exchange for the people whom you pay to be in your life or offer you a service, for example the milkman, hairdresser or professionals who currently help you such as counselors, therapists, nurses, psychiatrists etc.

The point of this is that we try to attain a balance of people across the circles, so that our lives don't revolve just around people who are paid to be in our lives! Don't worry if that is how it appears at the moment, just see it as an area that you need to pay attention to.

The people who support me the most include;

Their hopes about the possibilities for my future include:

The other people and considerations which need to be borne in mind when planning my future should include: (e.g.. family/carer view service changes, etc.)

My Circle of Support

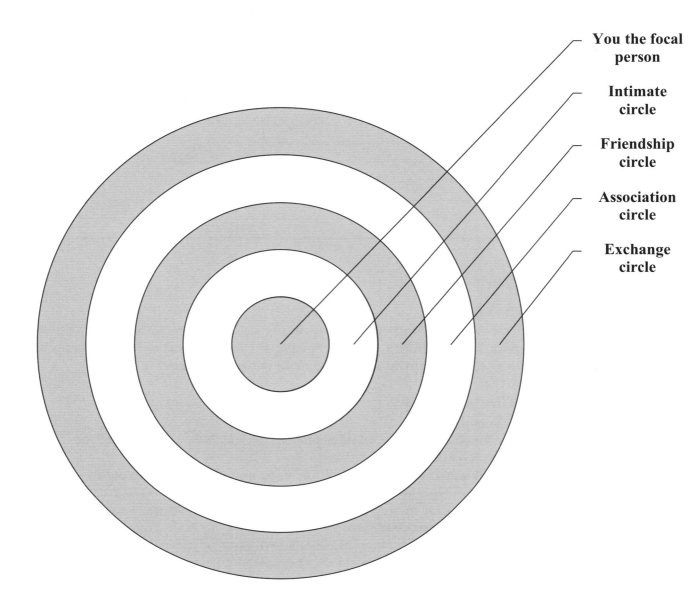

You the focal person

Intimate circle

Friendship circle

Association circle

Exchange circle

Part Ten - My Past / My current psychic distress
What I remember most about my past:

When I was a young child I:

When I was a teenager I:

What I remember about school is:

The friends I remember:

As I grow older I:

The people and places I remember are:

The important events in my life have been, (good, bad):

In the past, I have seen various professionals including:

The way in which professionals describe me is:

I agree (or disagree) with these comments because:

The things which I choose to continue talking about include:

My feeling today about these things are:

As a result of my previous experiences, the future should include / involve:

How I would describe my psychic distress:

Why I would say I am being assessed now:

What I want people who support me to know about my past and how it relates to my psychic distress:

How I cope:

What others can do to help me to cope and live well:

What doesn't help:

What I need and how I would like it provided:

Warning signs that show my levels of distress are increasing include:

The people I need to be contacted should my levels of distress increase are;

What I require them to do (practical help / support, e.g. feeding animals, looking after children) is:

Part Eleven - Choice / Control
The choices I feel I have:

Choices I would like to have:

Things I can do to extend my choices:

The level of control I currently experience over my life:

Things that affect my degree of control include:

Things I am doing to regain control include:

What I require should I lose control / go into crisis

Part Twelve - Risk and Safety
The things which seem to produce good results for me include:

The things which seem to lead to poor results for me include:

At present, if nothing were to change, my future would consist of:

Things I most fear happening include:

Things others seem to fear happening to me include:

How I feel right now:

How others feel regarding my distress right now:

Risk is a combination of three factors,
- **the potential severity of outcome**
- **the likelihood of that thing happening**
- **and how imminent that thing is actually perceived to be.**

It is important to remember that risk and the risk which we may present to ourselves or to other people is not just about us, it is also an issue for workers, organisations, our relatives and the public. For example other people will be concerned about self harm for a number of reasons; your safety obviously, but also the impact for and on them! The following table may prove helpful for you in discussions with workers regarding the risks everyone may be currently facing, and in agreeing common ground for how to keep all parties as safe as is possible.

What could happen? Who is at risk?	How severe or dangerous are the potential outcomes of this? 1 not serious for any party 5 very serious	How likely is this thing to happen? 1 low-5 high	When is this thing likely to happen? 1 distant-5 now	What should we do to manage the risks, to keep safe or reduce any potential harm?

Part Thirteen - My Future

Hopes and dreams for the future are an important part of recovery – they keep us going, motivate and encourage us.

The following should be considered in order of increased importance. The things at the top of the list, are those which will make the most important and meaningful difference to the quality of my life. So, when decisions are made for my individual plan, they should be made on the basis of how much impact they have on those things at the top of the list.

What I want now:

My dreams for the next two months include:

My dreams for the next six months include:

My hopes for what I'll be doing next year include:

My hopes for where I'll be in two years time include:

The THRIVE Assessment and Accomplishment Planning Tool - Summary

The following document should be written <u>with</u> the individual after their self assessment is complete. Its purpose is to construct a Recovery plan meaningful to the individual and all supporters involved. It is essentially a summary of the information gathered from the individual with detailed actions and practical support mechanisms which will support their recovery.

1. Who is the Person?

_____

_____

_____

_____

_____

_____

_____

_____

_____

_____

_____

_____

_____

2. Interdependence

3. Relationships

_____

_____

_____

_____

_____

_____

_____

_____

_____

_____

_____

_____

_____

_____

_____

_____

_____

_____

_____

_____

© crazydiamond

4. Recreation / what motivates the person?

_____

_____

_____

_____

_____

_____

_____

_____

_____

_____

_____

_____

_____

_____

_____

_____

_____

5. Meaningful Occupation / Work

6. Educational Goals

7. Physical Health Needs

8. Cultural / Spiritual Needs

_____

_____

_____

_____

_____

_____

_____

_____

_____

_____

_____

_____

_____

_____

_____

_____

_____

_____

9. Family / Friends

_____

_____

_____

_____

_____

_____

_____

_____

_____

_____

_____

_____

_____

_____

_____

_____

_____

_____

10. What is the life story?

11. Choice and Control issues

12. Risk and Safety Issues

_____

_____

_____

_____

_____

_____

_____

_____

_____

_____

_____

_____

_____

_____

_____

_____

_____

_____

_____

13. Hopes and Fears

Plan of Action for next six months – dated and signed by all involved

_____

_____

_____

_____

_____

_____

_____

_____

_____

_____

_____

_____

_____

_____

_____

_____

_____

_____

_____

Plan of Action should crisis arise – signed by all named and involved

_____

_____

_____

_____

_____

_____

_____

_____

_____

_____

_____

_____

_____

_____

_____

_____

_____

_____

Issues to be resolved / key problem areas

Other reading

Voice hearing
The Maastricht Interview with a Person who hears voices – Marius Romme
Working with Voices – Ron Coleman, Mike Smith

Self Harm
The Maastrich Interview with a person who self harms – Marius Romme
Self Harm Assessment of Risk and Safety (S.H.A.R.S.) - Mike Smith
Working with Self Harm - Mike Smith

Psychosis
Psychiatric First Aid in Psychosis – Ron Coleman, John Good, Mike Smith

Recovery
The THRIVE Approach to Wellness – Marion Aslan, Mike Smith
Working to Recovery – Ron Coleman, Paul Baker, Karen Taylor